WORLD IN
FOCUS

FOCUS ON FRANCE

CELIA TIDMARSH

WORLD ALMANAC® LIBRARY

Please visit our web site at: www.worldalmanaclibrary.com
For a free color catalog describing World Almanac® Library's list of high-quality books and multimedia programs, call 1-800-848-2928 (USA) or 1-800-387-3178 (Canada). World Almanac® Library's fax: (414) 332-3567.

Library of Congress Cataloging-in-Publication Data available upon request from publisher. Fax (414) 336-0157 for the attention of the Publishing Records Department.

ISBN 0-8368-6217-1 (lib. bdg.)
ISBN 0-8368-6236-8 (softcover)

This North American edition first published in 2006 by
World Almanac® Library
A Member of the WRC Media Family of Companies
330 West Olive Street, Suite 100
Milwaukee, WI 53212 USA

Commissioning editor: Victoria Brooker
Editor: Patience Coster
Inside design: Chris Halls, www.mindseyedesign.co.uk
Cover design: Hodder Wayland
Series concept and project management by EASI-Educational Resourcing (info@easi-er.co.uk)
Statistical research: Anna Bowden

World Almanac® Library editor: Alan Wachtel
World Almanac® Library cover design: Scott Krall

Population Density Map © 2003 UT-Battelle, LLC. All rights reserved.
Data for population density maps reproduced under licence from UT-Battelle, LLC.
All rights reserved.
Maps and graphs: Martin Darlison, Encompass Graphics

Picture acknowledgements:
The author and publisher would like to thank the following for allowing their pictures to be reproduced in this publication:
Corbis 8 (Archivo Iconografico, S. A.), 21 (Alex Grimm/Reuters), 22 (Brooks Kraft), 24 (Owen Franken), 34 (Reuters), 37 (Reuters), 44 (Fabrizio Bensch), 52 (Ken Straiton), 56 (Bossu Regis); EASI-Images/Edward Parker cover, 4, 5, 6, 9, 10, 11, 12, 13, 14, 15, 16, 17, 18, 19, 20, 23, 25, 26, 27, 28, 29, 30, 31, 32, 33, 35, 36, 38, 39, 40, 41, 42, 43, 45, 46 and title page, 47, 48, 49, 50, 51, 53, 54, 55, 57, 58 and 59.

The directional arrow portrayed on the map on page 7 provides only an approximation of north. The data used to produce the graphics and data panels in this title were the latest available at the time of production.

Printed in China

1 2 3 4 5 6 7 8 9 10 09 08 07 06

CONTENTS

Cover: The walled city of Carcassonne, southern France.

Title page: The traditional game of pétanque, or boules, is popular in France.

CHAPTER 1

France – An Overview

France is situated on the western edge of the European landmass. It is bordered by eight countries and has an extensive and varied coastline. France also governs eight overseas departments and territories located in the Caribbean, Indian, and Pacific Oceans.

THE PHYSICAL ENVIRONMENT

The physical landscape of France provides habitats for a wide variety of plants and animals. In general, France can be divided into two main regions. Toward the south and east are elevated plateaus and high mountains, including the Alps and the Pyrenees. Much of the north, west, and center of the country consists of broad plains and lowland hills and plateaus. Approximately 82 percent of the land area is made up of farmland or forests, which provide an important natural resource for France's economy. Until around 1945, a large proportion of the country's labor force—slightly less than one-third—still worked on the land.

ECONOMICS AND POPULATION

In 2003, France was ranked as one the world's wealthiest countries. It has the world's fifth largest economy, with strong industrial and technological sectors. During the second half of the twentieth century, agricultural employment in France declined rapidly. Today, the majority of France's workforce is employed in service industries and the professional and managerial sectors. France has a reputation for technological expertise and flair in areas such as the automobile and aircraft industries. Politically, France plays a key role in international politics, mainly through its membership in organizations such as the European Union (EU), the North Atlantic Treaty Organization (NATO), and the United Nations (UN).

Did You Know?

"La Marseillaise"—the French national anthem—is so named because soldiers from the southern city of Marseille sang it in the streets of Paris during the French Revolution.

◀ The Côte d'Azur, which is named after the azure blue of the Mediterranean Sea, is a spectacular rocky coastline with headlands, bays, and caves. The tops of the cliffs are covered with a form of sparse vegetation called maquis.

▲ The Eiffel Tower, built in 1889, is one of France's most famous landmarks. Located in the center of Paris, it was named after its designer, Gustave Eiffel.

In 2004, France's population was around 60.4 million. It has increased by about 18.6 million people since 1950. The country's population is of mixed origins, reflecting the long history of settlement in France by different groups. Among the most influential of these groups were the Gauls (a Celtic people) and the Franks (a group of Germanic tribes), who gave France its name. Since the mid-twentieth century, immigrants from France's former colonial territories, particularly those in Africa, and, more recently, from eastern Europe and Asia have settled in the country. The majority of French people (76 percent in 2005) live in urban areas. Paris, France's capital, dominates the country in both size and influence. France's settlements reflect their long history and represent a rich mix of architecture from Roman times through the present day.

Did You Know?

France is roughly the shape of a hexagon and is sometimes referred to by its inhabitants as "l'Hexagone."

HISTORY AND CULTURE

French history is characterized by numerous changes in territory and leadership, many of which resulted from lengthy and bloody wars. Under the leadership of King Louis XVI (ruled 1774–1792) and Emperor Napoléon I (ruled 1799–1815), for example, France's borders extended to include areas that are today part of the neighboring countries of Spain, Germany, and Italy. Between 1789 and 1794, the French Revolution transformed the country's system of government. This conflict helped to establish the principle of the constitutional republic by which France is now governed. France has also been invaded by foreign powers, most notably during World War I (1914–1918) and World War II (1939–1945). During both of these wars, some of the heaviest fighting took place on French soil.

France's rich cultural heritage has today spread far beyond its own borders. French food, fashion, art, movies, and architecture are world renowned for quality and innovation. The French language, which was the language of international diplomacy in the seventeenth and eighteenth centuries, also has an influence beyond France's boundaries and is spoken by many peoples around the world.

At the start of the twenty-first century, France's strong cultural and political position at the center of Europe is under pressure from other European nations and broader global forces. How France adapts to these global and regional changes will play a major role in determining its future.

▼ Paris is a lively cosmopolitan city with a thriving street culture. Its many public open spaces attract pavement artists, musicians, and jugglers.

Physical Geography Data

- Land area: 210,668 sq miles/545,630 sq km
- Water area: 541 sq miles/1,400 sq km
- Total area: 211,209 sq miles/547,030 sq km
- World rank (by area): 49
- Land boundaries: 1,794 miles/2,889 km
- Border countries: Andorra, Belgium, Germany, Italy, Luxembourg, Monaco, Spain, Switzerland
- Coastline: 2,128 miles/3,427 km
- Highest point: Mt. Blanc (15,771 ft/4,807 m)
- Lowest point: Rhone River Delta (-7 ft/-2 m)

Source: CIA World Factbook

 Did You Know?

Denim originates from the town of Nîmes in southern France. *Denim* is a contraction of *"de Nîmes,"* meaning "of Nîmes." The blue fabric was first manufactured in Nîmes in the eighteenth century and was exported to California during the 1840s by a man named Levi Strauss, who used it to make durable trousers for gold miners.

UNITED
KINGDOM

*English
Channel*

ATLANTIC
OCEAN

*Bay of
Biscay*

Calais
Dunkerque
Tourcoing
Boulogne-
sur-Mer
Lille
Roubaix
NORD-PAS-
DE-CALAIS

BELGIUM

GERMANY

LUXEMBOURG

HAUTE-
NORMANDIE
(UPPER
NORMANDY)

Amiens

PICARDIE

Aisne

Le Havre

Rouen

Reims

Metz

Caen

BASSE-
NORMANDIE
(LOWER NORMANDY)

PARIS
Versailles ★
ÎLE-DE-
FRANCE   *Seine*

LORRAINE
Nancy

Strasbourg

ALSACE

CHAMPAGNE-
ARDENNE

Mulhouse

Brest

BRETAGNE
(BRITTANY)

Rennes

Le Mans

Orléans

Dijon

Besançon

Belle Île

PAYS DE
LA LOIRE

Loire

BOURGOGNE

FRANCHE-
COMTE

SWITZERLAND

Angers
Tours

CENTRE

Nantes

Bourges

*Lake
Geneva*

Poitiers

F R A N C E

La Rochelle

POITOU-
CHARENTES

LIMOUSIN

Clermont-
Ferrand

Mont Blanc
4,807m
Villerbaune

Lyon

46°

Île d'Oleron

Limoges

RHONE-ALPES

Gironde

Saint-Etienne

AUVERGNE

Grenoble

ITALY

A L P S

Rhône

*Bay of
Biscay*

Bordeaux

Lot

*MASSIF
CENTRAL*

AQUITAINE

MIDI-
PYRENEES

PROVENCE-ALPES-
COTE D'AZUR

44°

Nîmes   Avignon

Nice   MONACO

Aix-en-
Provence

Cannes

Garonne

Toulouse

Montpellier

CAMARGUE

Marseille

Toulon

Pau

LANGUEDOC-
ROUSSILLON

*Golfe du
Lion*

Vignemale
3,298m
P Y R E N E E S
ANDORRA

Perpignan

SPAIN

*Mediterranean
Sea*

0   50   100 kilometers
0   50   100 miles

Bastia

CORSE
(CORSICA)

Ajaccio

Legend
★ Capital
● Cities > 500,000
● Cities > 200,000
• Cities > 100,000
· Other cities
▲ Mountain

CHAPTER 2

History

Prehistoric paintings in caves in the Périgord region of southwest France suggest that human settlement in France began in about 15,000 B.C. A more permanent record of human settlement, however, can be traced back to the period of the Gauls, a Celtic people from central Europe, who invaded the area in about 1500 B.C. They settled in a region that became known as Gaul and developed trading links with the Greeks, who had colonies on the Mediterranean coast.

In 52 B.C., the Gauls were defeated by troops of the Roman emperor Julius Caesar. The Roman Empire controlled Gaul until the fifth century A.D., when it came under attack by tribes from northern Europe. One of these tribes, the Franks, eventually took control of the area and named it "la Francie."

The Frankish king, Charlemagne, ruled from A.D. 771 to 814 and expanded the French Empire into parts of Spain, Germany, and northern Italy. Following Charlemagne's death, the French Empire was divided among his heirs. In 911, the Normans, a group of Scandinavian conquerors, took control of the area in northern France now known as Normandy. Other areas, such as Anjou, were taken over by the English. By 987, the Franks still ruled the kingdom of France, but at that time, this was just the small area that is now the Île de France region.

CLAIMS TO THE THRONE

When William, duke of Normandy, invaded England in 1066, he seized areas of France that were under English rule. In 1154, Henry II took the English throne. Henry II's marriage to Eleanor of Aquitaine, the former queen of France, gave him control of large areas of southwest France. Following this, long periods of conflict between the English and the French

◄ The Pont du Gard is an exceptionally well preserved Roman aqueduct located near Avignon in southern France. It was once part of a 31-mile (50 km) long system of canals constructed around 19 B.C. to bring water from near Uzès to Nîmes. The Pont du Gard has thirty-five arches in its upper tier.

occurred. In 1328, Charles IV of France died with no obvious heir. His nephew, the English king Edward III, was enraged when the French throne was given to Charles's grandson, Philippe de Valois.

Edward's claim to the French throne led to the Hundred Years' War (1337–1453). For much of this war, the English had the upper hand, defeating the French at the Battle of Agincourt in 1415 and taking control of Paris in 1420. In 1429, however, a young peasant girl named Joan of Arc claimed that God had told her to urge the French troops to victory. She is credited with turning the war in France's favor by inspiring French soldiers with her divine

Did You Know?

In Brittany, standing stones and burial mounds dating from between 5700 B.C. and 1000 B.C. have been found around the town of Carnac.

message. In 1429, Charles VII was crowned king of France, and in 1436, the French recaptured Paris. By 1453, the English had been driven from most French territory.

INFLUENCES OF RENAISSANCE AND RELIGION

Between 1494 and 1559, France waged wars with Italy over territory. At this time, a the Renaissance was taking place in Italy. During the reign of Francis I (1515–1547), many Italian ideas about culture were brought to France. Francis I invited the Italian artist Leonardo da Vinci to France, and the artist brought with him the *Mona Lisa*, a famous painting that still hangs in the Louvre museum in Paris today.

▼ The Cathedral of Notre Dame in Paris took more than 180 years to build. Completed in 1345, it was one of the first cathedrals built in the Gothic style, which is characterized by many elaborate features, such as flying buttresses and stained glass windows.

Between 1562 and 1598, the Wars of Religion took place between Huguenots (French Protestants) and Catholics. In 1598, King Henry IV ended these wars by passing the Edict of Nantes, a law that granted religious freedom to all French subjects.

FROM THE BOURBONS TO REVOLUTION

Between 1598 and 1792, France was ruled by the Bourbon dynasty. One of its greatest leaders was King Louis XIV (ruled 1643–1715), who led France to become the dominant power in Europe. Louis waged military campaigns to gain new French territories, such as Canada and the Louisiana territory in North America. Under Louis XIV, a period of industrialization and innovation took place in France. The king used France's wealth to build a vast chateau at Versailles, to which he relocated the royal court from Paris. Toward the end of his reign, Louis involved France in the disastrous War of the Spanish Succession (1701–1714), an attempt to establish a Bourbon king on the Spanish throne. Other European countries, including England and Italy, opposed this extension of French power. In 1714, the Treaty of Utrecht ended the war by allowing the Bourbon king Philip V to take the Spanish throne if he broke his connection with the French throne.

France suffered further military defeats under Louis XV (ruled 1715–1774). These included the loss of French colonies in Canada, the West Indies, and India to the British. Louis XVI (ruled 1774–1792) tried to avenge the loss of these territories by siding with the United States against Britain in the American Revolution (1778–1783). The French people were heavily taxed to pay for this expensive military venture, and this resulted in widespread poverty in France. These conditions contributed to a growing resentment of the country's ruling elite.

◀ King Louis XIV moved his court to the Chateau de Versailles in 1682. Versailles is about 12 miles (19.3 kilometers) from the center of Paris.

▲ In this nineteenth-century painting, royalist troops battle to defend the Bastille prison in Paris from angry crowds on July 14, 1789.

By 1789, public unrest had erupted into a popular revolution. The people formed the National Assembly, which refused to disband until a constitution was drawn up giving rights to ordinary French citizens. On July 14, the king's troops attempted to disperse the Assembly, but their action backfired. Crowds stormed the Bastille, a prison in Paris that was a symbol of the oppressive rule of the king. A period of great bloodshed followed, and many "enemies of the Revolution," including nobles and the king and queen, were beheaded. By 1792, France had a new constitution and was declared a republic. A period of social unrest during which many people suspected of opposing the Revolution were assassinated, however, continued until 1794. A new form of parliamentary government emerged from this period, but public distrust of the new political leaders lingered. Against this background, Napoléon Bonaparte came to power in 1799.

? Did You Know?

The guillotine was a machine designed to behead privileged nobles, including members of the royal family, during the French Revolution of 1789. Large crowds would gather to watch the public executions.

▲ Napoléon Bonaparte commissioned the Arc de Triomphe in 1806 to commemorate his military victories. Napoléon, however, began to lose battles, and, by 1813, he was no longer emperor of France. The Arc was completed in the 1830s. It is one of the main landmarks in Paris, located at the meeting point of twelve broad avenues.

NAPOLÉON BONAPARTE

Napoléon Bonaparte was a general in the French army during the Revolution. In 1799, he took control of the government in a military coup and, in the following years, consolidated his power through military actions against Austria and Britain. In 1804, Napoléon declared himself emperor of France. By 1812, his armies controlled most of western and central mainland Europe. Napoléon's invasion of Russia in 1812, however, ended in defeat. Several nations formed an alliance against France, and Napoléon was defeated at the Battle of the Nations at Leipzig, Germany, in 1813, after which he was forced into exile.

In 1815, Napoléon returned to France and ruled for a further "Hundred Days" before he was again defeated, this time by the British, in the Battle of Waterloo. He was exiled to the remote island of St. Helena, where he died in 1824. Still remembered by many French people as a national hero, Napoléon made important changes to the government of France. For example, he ensured that the legal system incorporated principles from the French Revolution, such as the recognition of an individual's right to own property.

THE WORLD WARS

France was invaded during World War I (1914–1918). More than one million young French soldiers were killed in the trenches during this war, and large areas of northwest

France, including farmland and villages, were devastated. During World War II (1939–1945), France was occupied by Germany in 1940. It was liberated in 1944 by the combined forces of the Allies and the Free French.

France's Fourth Republic (1946–1958) was founded following World War II and lasted until 1958, when a war of independence in the French colony of Algeria caused a crisis. This war had begun in 1954. By 1956, more than 400,000 French troops were fighting in Algeria with no sign of an end to the conflict. As members of the government led by President René Coty argued among themselves about what to do, other politicians and army officers staged a coup. Coty was replaced by a former French president, General Charles de Gaulle, who established the Fifth Republic in 1958 and brought the war to an end in 1962.

PEACE AND PROSPERITY

After World War II, the French government adopted economic and political policies to restore prosperity and peace. One of the most ambitious of these was the joint creation with Germany of the European Coal and Steel Community in 1951. This early trading agreement later evolved and expanded to become the European Economic Community (EEC) in 1957, a group that was renamed the European Union in 1993. By 2005, twenty-five countries belonged to the EU.

The prosperity enjoyed by France over the last fifty years can—in part, at least—be attributed to the success of these institutions. Whether the

expanded EU will continue to serve France's future so well remains to be seen. In May 2005, the French people seemed to have lost faith in the EU when they voted against the proposed EU constitution. This outcome led to the resignation of Prime Minister Jean Pierre Raffarin and to much debate between and within the other member countries of the EU.

Focus on: The French Republics

In France, transitions between republics have been brought about by political upheavals such as the period of absolute rule between the First and Second Republics or the coup to remove the president between the Fourth and Fifth Republics. Each of France's republics is marked by changes to the constitution, although the basic principles of the French Revolution have remained in place since the First Republic. The dates of France's five republics are:

First Republic 1792–1804
Second Republic 1848–1852
Third Republic 1870–1940
Fourth Republic 1946–1958
Fifth Republic 1958–present

▶ Hundreds of cemeteries in northern France are filled with the graves of people who died in World War I.

CHAPTER 3

Landscape and Climate

France is Europe's third largest country (after Russia and the Ukraine), covering an area of 210,668 sq miles (545,630 sq km). It is approximately twice the size of Britain or Colorado. The country shares land borders with seven countries and is bounded by the Atlantic Ocean to the west, the Mediterranean Sea to the south, and the English Channel (*La Manche*) to the north.

MASSIFS AND MOUNTAINS

France's physical landscape ranges from low, rolling plains to high rugged mountains. While about 60 percent of France is below 820 feet (250 meters) in altitude, the remaining 40 percent is a spectacular highland landscape.

The oldest of the highlands are the massifs, which formed between 345 million and 225 million years ago. The Massif Central covers about 35,135 sq miles (91,000 sq km) of south-central France and is famous for its chain of extinct volcanoes, which includes the 4,806-foot (1,465 m) high Puy de Dôme. Other mountainous regions in France include the Alps, the Jura, and the Pyrenees. Formed fifty million years ago, these mountains are geologically younger than the massifs and are more rugged and higher. The French Alps include Mont Blanc which, at 15,771 feet (4,807 m), is the highest peak in Europe. The Pyrenees reach a maximum height of 11,168 feet (3,404 m), and the Jura reach 5,653 feet (1,723 m).

◀ The landscape of France is varied and includes high plateaus, such as the one shown in the background of this photograph; rugged mountains; and vast, rolling plains.

▲The Loire River rises in the Cévennes and drains into the Bay of Biscay. The section shown here flows through the town of Amboise.

RIVERS AND COASTS

France is drained by five large river systems. The Loire is its longest river, stretching 629 miles (1,012 km) from the Massif Central to the Atlantic coast. The Garonne also flows into the Atlantic, with tributaries draining much of southwest France, including the Pyrenees. The Rhône links Lake Geneva in the Alps with the Mediterranean Sea, and it is joined at Lyon by the River Saône. The country's remaining two major river systems are the Rhine, which forms part of the border between France and Germany, and the Seine, which passes through Paris before draining into the English Channel.

France has an immensely varied coastline that is about 2,128 miles (3,427 km) long. It features salt marshes around the estuary of the Rhône on the Mediterranean coast, sand dunes on the Atlantic coast south of Bordeaux, chalk cliffs on the Normandy coast, and rocky beaches both in Brittany and on the Cote d'Azur. The fan-shaped mouth of the Rhône, the point at which it flows into the Mediterranean, is a fine example of a delta.

? Did You Know?

The official height of Mont Blanc varies because of the changing thickness of the ice and snow on its highest peak. It was measured at 15,771 feet (4,807 m) in 1894; 15,782 feet (4,810 m) in 2001; and again at 15,771 feet in 2004.

VARIATIONS IN THE CLIMATE

In general, France has a temperate climate with mild winters, although variations in climate do exist within the country as a result of the proximity of the sea. Western France is usually wetter because the prevailing winds bring moisture from the Atlantic Ocean. Also, during the winter months, warm ocean currents pass close to the country's west coast so temperatures there are higher than those in inland regions. Eastern France can be very cold in winter and very hot in summer. This is because the vast European landmass heats up and cools down more quickly than the sea. Altitude is also an influence on climate in France. Mountainous areas are generally cooler because the temperature falls by about 1.8 °Fahrenheit (1 °Celsius) for every 492 feet (150 m) of altitude. This is known as the lapse rate. Northern France is situated between latitudes 42°N and 52°N, which makes it generally cooler than the south.

EXTREME WEATHER AND CLIMATIC EVENTS

Extreme weather and climatic events do not occur very frequently in France but can cause problems in the country on occasion. In 2003, for example, much of France experienced a summer with a record-breaking heatwave and the worst drought in twenty-five years. This was followed, in the southeastern regions of the country, by serious winter flooding that was caused by torrential rainfall.

The events of 2003 would normally be considered rare by climatologists, and it was unusual that they occurred in the same year. Some climatologists believe that such extreme climatic events are becoming more frequent

▼ Dairy cattle graze in the lush, green pastures of Normandy, in northern France, where the climate is generally wetter than in the south.

because of global warming. Possible reasons other than global warming, however, exist. In southeastern France, for example, the clearing of natural vegetation to build more houses and roads is thought to have reduced the ability of the ground to absorb water during periods of heavy rainfall. Instead, rain flowed rapidly into rivers that could not handle more water.

▲ Vines grow in the sunny and generally frost-free southern regions of France.

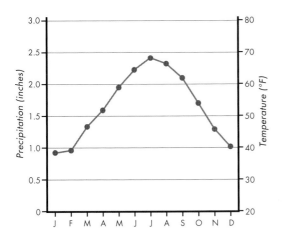

▲ Average monthly climate conditions in Paris

Focus on: The Mistral

The Mistral is a wind that blows down the Rhône Valley for about one hundred days each year, usually in winter and early spring. It is a katabatic wind, or a wind caused when cold, dense air from mountainous areas flows downhill and replaces the relatively warm, light air in lower-lying valleys. In the case of the Mistral, cold air from the Massif Central spills into the Rhône Valley and is channeled southward to the Mediterranean. The Mistral is a cold, dry, gusty wind that occasionally can damage buildings and uproot trees. Some people in France believe the Mistral affects people's moods because some who live in its path often report having headaches and feeling depressed and irritable.

CHAPTER 4

Population and Settlements

In 2004, the French population was about 60.4 million, with an additional 1.7 million people living in overseas territories. Between 1950 and 1980, the population surged from 41.8 million to 53.8 million. In common with other western European countries, this growth has slowed as the fertility rate (the average number of children born to each woman) has fallen. In 1964, it was just under 3, but by 2001, it had fallen to 1.9. This trend, combined with higher life expectancy, has led to a gradual aging of the population; an increasing proportion of France's population is over sixty-five years old.

AN AGING POPULATION

Today, 16 percent of France's population is over sixty-five, and this figure is expected to rise to 33 percent by 2040. The government is concerned about the demands that an aging population will place on health and social services. The ratio of the working-age population, which generates taxes to pay for health and social services, to the older, retired population is declining. This situation may be improved by people working beyond the official retirement age of sixty or by a future change in the retirement age to extend people's working lives. Also, modern technology and industry are more productive than they once were. It is possible that fewer workers will be able to generate the same or greater incomes and be able to support the aging population.

▼ In general, French people over age sixty-five are in better health than people of their age were in the past. In retirement, they may have more time to pursue leisure interests and to socialize.

A MIX OF PEOPLES

France's population includes people from many different origins, reflecting a long history of immigration to the country. During the twentieth century, France allowed two main phases of immigration to meet the need for labor. After World War I, many people were allowed to migrate to France from other European countries, such as Italy and Poland, to fill the gap that the war deaths had left in the workforce. There was a similar need following World War II, although this time immigrants came mainly from Portugal and North African countries such as Tunisia and Algeria that were once French colonies. Since 1974, unemployment in France has been rising, and France has placed stricter controls on immigration. Most of the immigrants allowed entry to France since 1974 have been people with close family members already in the country.

When immigrants become citizens of France, they are considered to have shed their cultural differences. For this reason, no official records are kept of immigrants' countries of origin, and there are no government statistics showing how many immigrants have settled in France. Despite this policy of assimilation, differences do exist. For example, immigrants from North Africa brought Islam to France, and there are now at least six million Muslims in France. Music and food from North Africa are also enjoyed by the wider French society.

Cultural and religious differences are the focus of occasional tensions between ethnic minority groups and French extremists. In 2002, these tensions became national news when Jean-Marie Le Pen, leader of the right-wing Le Front National (National Front) party, gained some support in presidential elections for his promise to completely end immigration into France. He and his followers blamed immigration for high unemployment, even though immigrants to France usually take on the low-paid unskilled jobs that other French citizens do not want. Ultimately, Le Pen lacked enough support to win the presidency.

▲ France's mix of people of many ethnic origins is evident on the streets of Paris, a city in which many immigrants from different cultures live and work.

❓ Did You Know?

Ethnic minorities in France are more likely to suffer social problems than the majority population. Young North Africans in France, for example, have a 40 percent unemployment rate compared to 10 percent for young-adult members of the majority population.

WHERE PEOPLE LIVE

On average, population density in France is 286 people per sq mile (110 per sq km). There are huge variations between regions, however, and highly urbanized areas, such as Paris, are far more densely populated than rural areas, such as the Auvergne. About 40 percent of France is sparsely populated and suffers from economic and social problems such as lack of jobs and services (for example, hospitals and post offices). The most affected areas run in a band from the northeast to the southwest regions of France, known as the "empty diagonal." These areas are declining further as young people migrate to regions that offer more opportunities. The government is trying to tackle these problems by encouraging jobs and income generation. One example of this is the availability of government grants for people who want to convert disused farm buildings into second homes.

In France, any settlement with a population of more than five thousand is classified as urban. By this definition, around 76 percent of the population lives in urban areas. Today, many of the largest cities are losing their populations to nearby villages and smaller towns. This is because many people want to escape the stresses of city life, such as air pollution and traffic congestion. Improved public transportation means that many of those leaving the city still commute to city jobs, but others are finding new employment in their home settlements. Some villages have adopted strategies to encourage this trend. For example, Neuvy-le-Roi, near Tours, has turned part of its school into a center for small-scale, local businesses and services. This program has helped create 150 jobs in five years.

Did You Know?

The region of the Île de France, in which Paris is located, covers only 2 percent of France's area but is home to 20 percent of the country's population.

▲ This photo of Annecy, in the central part of southeastern France, shows the traditional older style of housing typical of many French towns and cities.

Population Data

- Population: 60.4 million
- Population 0–14 yrs: 19%
- Population 15–64 yrs: 65%
- Population 65+ yrs: 16%
- Population growth rate: 0.5%
- Population density: 286 per sq mile/ 110.4 per sq km
- Urban population: 76%
- Major cities: Lyon 1,408,000
              Marseille 1,384,000
              Paris 9,854,000

Source: United Nations and World Bank

◀ Although most of France's people live in towns and cities, the country still has many villages in rural areas. This one in southern France has old, traditionally styled houses clustered around a church.

With a population of around 2 million in its older central area and a further 7.8 million in its wider metropolitan area, Paris is France's largest city. The growth of Paris has caused problems, such as serious traffic congestion. Since the 1960s, various urban development programs have encouraged the relocation of offices and services away from the central area to relieve congestion. The new national library, for example, is located in Tolbiac, a previously underdeveloped district of eastern Paris.

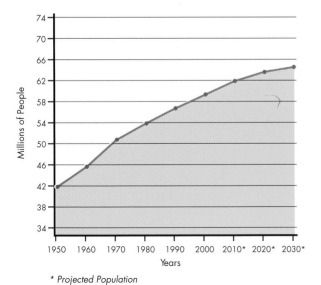

▲ Population growth, 1950–2030

* Projected Population

Focus on: Problems of Urban Deprivation

Between 1950 and 1970, many immigrants arriving to work in France were housed in estates that were built quickly and cheaply. Most of this housing consisted of high-rise apartment buildings on the edges of cities such as Marseille and Lyon. These estates, such as the Petit Bard estate in Montpellier, are now run-down because they have had little maintenance work since they were built. Their populations are still mostly made up of the immigrants—mainly North Africans—who first settled there, and they have some of the highest unemployment rates, lowest incomes, and lowest levels of literacy (as low as 66 percent) in France.

CHAPTER 5

Government and Politics

France is a democratic republic, with an elected president and Parliament, which is made up of the National Assembly and the Senate. The National Assembly is the main decision-making body, while the Senate's power is limited. The president is elected to a five-year term, as are the 577 deputies who make up the National Assembly.

As head of state, the president holds considerable power, particularly in relation to foreign policy. He or she chooses the prime minister, although the latter must be selected from deputies who represent the majority party in the National Assembly. As head of the government, the prime minister then chooses the government ministers.

The president and prime minister may represent different political parties. From 1997 to 2002, President Jacques Chirac of the right-wing l'Union Pour un Movement Populaire (Union for a Popular Movement) worked alongside Prime Minister Lionel Jospin of the left-wing La Parti Socialiste (Socialist Party). This situation is known in France as "cohabitation."

LOCAL GOVERNMENT

The local government of France is divided into five tiers. There are 22 *régions* (regions) that are divided into 100 *départements*

▼ The Palais de Luxembourg, located in Paris, was built in 1631. It is now home to the French Senate.

◀ The National Assembly meets in Paris. Members take seats to the left or right of the center of the groups' semi-circular chamber, according to their political allegiance.

(departments), further divided into 342 *arrondisements*. The two smallest tiers are the 4,054 *cantons* and the 36,763 *communes*. Traditionally, France's central government has appointed a *prefect* (leader) to head the various départements. In 1982, 1986, and 2003, however, changes were made to the law as part of a process of decentralization. Today, much of the prefect's power over transportation, tourism, economic development, and education has been transferred to locally elected departmental councils. These councils are entitled to call referenda on local issues to give people more say in their government.

POLITICAL PARTIES

There is a wide range of political parties in France, from far left to far right. For general elections, parties will often merge into coalitions to increase their support base. At the time of the 1997 election, for example, a coalition called the *gauche plurielle* (the broad left) was formed by the Socialists, the Greens, and other left-wing parties.

Since 1958, when the present constitution was adopted, there have been both right- and left-wing presidents and governments. Until recently, popular support tended to favor the middle ground of politics rather than the extremes of left or right. In the presidential election of 2002, Jean-Marie Le Pen, leader of the far-right party Le Front National, was voted through to the second round of the election to face Jacques Chirac. In between the first and second round elections, many French people took to the streets to demonstrate against Le Pen and his racist policies. In the second round, Chirac won by the largest margin ever recorded at this stage of a French presidential election.

? Did You Know?

France has four *régions d'outre-mer* (overseas regions) that hold the same status as metropolitan French regions. They are Guadeloupe, French Guiana, Martinique, and Réunion.

THE CONSTITUTION

The French constitution draws on principles from the *Declaration of the Rights of Man*, a document written in 1789 by radicals during the Revolution. The constitution establishes France as a secular and democratic republic. It also promotes a strong sense of French identity, stating that all citizens are equal, regardless of origin, race, religion, culture, or language. Sometimes elements of the constitution can cause problems. For example, it is stated that the republic's language is French. This means there is no official recognition of regional languages in areas like Brittany and Corsica. Since the start of the Fifth Republic in 1958, the constitution has been amended several times. In 1997, for example, the government approved equal representation for men and women in political posts. While the percentage of women in the National Assembly has doubled since 1996, it is still low. In 2002, only 12 percent of the deputies were women.

Focus on: Referendum in Corsica

In 2003, Corsica held a referendum on whether to accept greater independence from France. It was hoped that a "yes" outcome would end more than thirty years of violent campaigns, including bombings and the murder of a government prefect, carried out by groups demanding independence from France. Although those carrying out the violence are a small minority, the people of Corsica have a strong sense of regional identity. For a long time, the French government's view has been that granting autonomy or independence to Corsica would undermine the constitution and threaten the unity of France. In recognition of the general trend toward decentralization, however, President Chirac changed his mind and gave his support to the referendum proposal. The outcome of the vote was extremely close, with 50.98 percent voting against independence.

▼ A local politician campaigns for votes in Corsica. A small minority of Corsicans oppose the dominance of French language and culture and want independence from France.

FRANCE AND THE EU

As a founding member of the European Union, France has influenced and been influenced by various EU policies. French governments and the French people have generally been positive about the role the EU plays in political and economic life. In 2002, France adopted the EU's currency, known as the Euro. Sometimes, however, conflict occurs between France and the EU. In 1999, for example, France signed the European Charter on Regional and Minority Languages. In spite of this, France's highest court, the Conseil Constitutionel, ruled that the charter conflicted with France's constitution, which states that the Republic's language is French.

The enlargement of the EU, from fifteen to twenty-five countries in 2004, is challenging France's role within it. Other countries are applying for membership. In particular, Turkey's application to join the EU is opposed by about two thirds of French voters, partly because of fears that Turkish immigrants will take jobs from French citizens.

French people seemed to be turning against the EU when, in May 2005, 55 percent voted in a referendum to reject the proposed EU constitution. Some analysts believe this outcome had more to do with voters wanting to show their disapproval of domestic policies, such as the reform of the health care system, rather than an outright rejection of the principles of the EU. The result of the French referendum, however, has raised questions about the future of the EU and France's position within it.

▼ Like some other economically developed countries, France has many immigrants who do unskilled, low-paid jobs that are essential to the economy. Some French voters fear that their jobs might be lost to immigrant workers.

CHAPTER 6

Energy and Resources

France is a highly industrialized country, and it accounts for about 2.5 percent of the world's total energy consumption. Since 1980, the consumption rate has risen steadily, from 8.5 quadrillion BTU (quads) to 10.5 quads in 2001. France's energy consumption, at 178 million BTU per person, is high compared with neighboring western European countries, such as Britain, which uses 142 million BTU per person. It is still, however, much lower than that of the United States, which consumes 342 million BTU per person.

THE PROBLEM OF DEPENDENCY

France has few natural energy resources. Until the 1970s, coal provided about 20 percent of the country's primary, or total, fuel needs and 46 percent of its generated electricity. France's coal reserves, however, are now either exhausted or too expensive to access at present, and its last mines were closed in 2004. France's primary energy requirements are now met by oil, nuclear energy, and natural gas.

Until the mid 1970s, oil provided 77 percent and nuclear energy only 5 percent of France's energy. When oil producers increased their prices in 1973, the French government reduced oil imports and increased its use of nuclear energy. Uranium was mined in France, so the country had more control over this energy source. Domestic uranium deposits are now greatly depleted, but nuclear energy is still regarded as a relatively independent energy source. French companies mine deposits in Niger, Canada, Australia, and Kazakhstan, so France still has some control over this vital resource. In 2004, France was using 2.04 million barrels of oil a day (bbl/d), of which 1.96 million bbl/d were imported from Saudi Arabia and Norway. About 97 percent of the natural gas consumed in France is imported from Norway, Russia, and Algeria.

▼ France imports crude oil and gas and refines them for different uses within the country. This oil refinery is at Dunkerque on France's northern coast.

Energy Data

- Energy consumption as % of world total: 2.5%
- Energy consumption by sector (% of total):
    Industry: 30
    Transportation: 31
    Agriculture: 2
    Services: 13
    Residential: 24
- CO_2 emissions as % of world total: 1.6
- CO_2 emissions per capita in tons per year: 6.7

Source: World Resources Institute

THE NUCLEAR ENERGY DILEMMA

France has the second largest nuclear power capacity in the world, second only to the United States. Nuclear energy provides 81 percent of the country's electricity. The electricity it produces is relatively cheap and exceeds the country's needs, so France exports electricity to neighboring countries. France is now the largest electricity exporter in the European Union.

A benefit of nuclear energy, as opposed to fossil fuels, is that it does not release greenhouse gases (carbon, sulphur dioxide, and nitrous oxides) when burned. The French public, however, is increasingly worried about the safety of nuclear energy, particularly the disposal of radioactive waste. The government had planned for nuclear power to generate all of the country's electricity, but this plan is being reconsidered as public opposition to nuclear power grows.

▲ This nuclear power station is in the Rhone-Alpes region of central southeastern France.

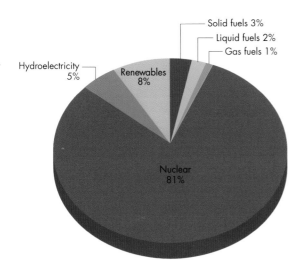

▲ Energy generation by source

Focus on: Renewable Energy

With the exception of hydroelectric power (HEP), renewable energy sources have yet to be commercially developed in France. The goal set by the government is to provide 21 percent of the country's energy from renewable sources by 2010. HEP currently provides 5 percent, but its potential has already been fully developed in areas where the natural conditions are suitable to it, such as the fast-flowing rivers of the Massif Central. A tidal barrage to generate electricity has been built across the Rance estuary in Normandy. In 2001, power from geothermal, biomass, solar, and wind sources accounted for less than 1 percent of France's energy use. With more investment from the French government and companies, there is room for development of all these energy sources.

MINERAL RESOURCES

France used to be an important producer of iron ore, bauxite, uranium, and coal. By 2004, however, mining of these minerals in the country had ceased. Increased imports of cheaper raw materials, lower prices as a result of competition, and the depletion of mineral reserves all contributed to the closure of French mines. Another factor was the removal of subsidies by the French government as a result of EU policies. Subsidies had artificially been keeping unprofitable mines open.

FORESTRY

Timber is an important natural resource in France, and forests cover 22.9 million acres (9.3 million hectares)—approximately 17 percent of the country's land area. Two-thirds of the forests are deciduous, and they include beech and oak. Pine is the most common coniferous tree in France's forests. The Office Nationale des Forêts (ONF) manages Frances's national forests. The annual harvest from nationally owned forests is about 1,200 cubic feet (34 million cubic meters) of timber. About 70 percent of France's forests are owned and managed privately.

Environmentalists criticize the ONF for giving the commercial use of timber a higher priority than conservation. Forests also provide beautiful natural environments that are enjoyed by tourists and generate tourist revenue.

▼ Logging operations such as this one near Montauban provide jobs in rural areas where there may be few other types of employment available.

▲ Small fishing boats, such as these vessels at St. Brieuc, in Brittany, are owned and operated by individuals or families rather than big companies.

FISHING

Fish consumption per person in France rose steadily from about 33 pounds (15 kilograms) in the 1970s to 57 pounds (26 kg) in the late 1990s. France's fisheries produce about 826,725 tons (750,000 metric tons) per year, with a value of 0.14 percent of the gross domestic product (GDP). This small percentage conceals the importance of fishing as an economic activity in coastal regions. More than eight thousand vessels in the fishing fleets work around the coasts of France and its overseas départements and territories. French fleets fish off the eastern coast of Canada because two islands—Saint-Pierre and Miquelon— remain French territory.

The operation and range of French fishing fleets are affected by European Union policies and international agreements. Introduced in 1983, the Common Fisheries Policy requires that member states conserve and manage fish stocks. France has also signed international agreements, including those creating Exclusive Economic Zones (EEZs). These are maritime areas of 200 nautical miles (370 km) from the coast in which the coastal state has rights over the living resources of the sea. Until the EEZs, it was assumed that the ocean's resources should be free for all to use. The EEZ over which France has rights covers 4.2 million sq miles (11 million sq km), made up of 100,386 sq miles (260,000 sq km) around metropolitan France and over 4 million sq miles (10 million sq km) around overseas départements and territories.

 Did You Know?

Bauxite, the ore from which aluminum is smelted, is named after Les Baux, which is located near Arles, in southern France. Bauxite was first discovered there in 1821.

CHAPTER 7

Economy and Income

France is the world's fifth largest economy, with a Gross National Income (GNI) of U.S.$1.5 trillion. Its economic strength is built upon a highly skilled workforce, a range of manufacturing industries, and substantial agricultural resources. The country's service sector is its largest employer, providing over 72 percent of France's jobs (having risen from 58 percent in 1980). Since 1980, employment in manufacturing has declined from 33 percent to 25 percent, and agriculture now provides only 3 percent of jobs in France, compared with nearly 9 percent in 1980. Imported minerals, such as uranium, are still processed in France, and this provides some jobs, although it employs less than 1 percent of France's workforce.

SERVICE SECTOR

The expanding service sector includes banking, insurance, architecture, transportation, education, and health care. Tourism is a major service industry. France is one of the world's most popular tourist destinations, with 75 million foreign visitors arriving in 2003 and generating U.S.$64.5 billion. France also has successful high-technology and telecommunications industries. The French government finances about 48 percent of these industries' research.

MANUFACTURING

In France, jobs have been lost in traditional manufacturing industries, such as ship-building, because of competition from countries such as South Korea and China, where labor costs are lower. Also, domestic raw materials, such as iron ore, have been

▼ In France's industrial heartlands, heavy goods are still transported by barge.

exhausted, which has led to the closure of many of the industries dependent on them. Some economically important industries in France, however, still thrive. France is the world's third major car manufacturer; its two major car companies, Peugeot-Citroën and Renault, produced 5.5 million vehicles in 2001. Much of the steel used in these cars is produced in France, and other French companies supply car parts. Tires, for example, are supplied by Michelin, which is based in Clermont-Ferrand. The aeronautics company Matra-Aérospatiale, which is part of the European Airbus consortium, is also successful. In 2003, it sold more than three hundred Airbus planes, overtaking Boeing as the largest producer of civil aircraft.

AGRICULTURE

The number of people employed in France in agriculture has declined. In the past, many French people worked the land. Over the past forty years, this has changed, largely as a result of the EU's Common Agricultural Policy (CAP). CAP encouraged increased mechanization and use of fertilizers. These changes led to higher production with fewer people needed to work the land. France is the world's second largest food producer, second only to the United States. Over 70 percent of France's agricultural output is processed, and its foodstuffs industry is the country's third largest employer.

Economic Data

📂 Gross National Income (GNI) in U.S.$: 1.5 trillion

📂 World rank by GNI: 5

📂 GNI per capita in U.S.$: 24,770

📂 World rank by GNI per capita: 23

📂 Economic growth: 0.1%

Source: World Bank

▲ A worker on a Renault assembly line in Romorantin in central France.

Did You Know?

As a member of the EU, about 70 percent of France's trade is with other EU countries.

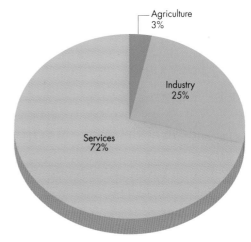

- Agriculture 3%
- Industry 25%
- Services 72%

▲ Contribution by sector to national income

▲ A wine chemist at work. In France today, working women generally have better academic qualifications than their male counterparts.

UNEMPLOYMENT

Although France has a strong economy, the country also has some economic problems. Unemployment is higher in France than in many other European Union countries. In 2002, the unemployment rate was 8.8 percent, compared with 5.2 percent in Britain and 2.9 percent in the Netherlands. Since 1980, unem-ployment for people under twenty-five years old has risen from 15.5 percent to 21 percent.

The government has tried to solve the country's unemployment problem by introducing a thirty-five-hour work week. It hoped to create more jobs by restricting the hours of those already working. Although more than 200,000

jobs were created between 1997 and 2000, some economists have argued that the thirty-five-hour work week has actually worsened overall unemployment in the country by making France less competitive in the global economy. In 2005, in spite of the fact that 69 percent of the French public opposed the change, France's government voted to increase the work week to forty-eight hours. Workers are not legally required to work forty-eight hours a week, but now companies can demand that they do.

 Did You Know?

On January 1, 2002, France, along with most other countries in the EU, dropped its national currency in favor of the Euro. Twelve of the twenty-five EU countries have adopted the Euro, and many of the newest EU members, who joined in 2004, have applied for adoption.

REGIONAL INEQUALITIES

Significant economic differences exist between the various geographical areas in France. The four largest urban areas—Paris, Lyon, Marseille, and Lille —have 42 percent of the country's population and a high share of its total economic activity. In contrast, many rural areas in the south and southeast are suffering from economic decline. Traditionally, these rural areas were dependent on farming, but in France as a whole, the number of farms declined from 1,017,000 in 1988 to about 664,000 in 2000. When older farmers retire, no one takes over their farms because younger people are moving to more prosperous areas in search of work. The economic problems of poor rural areas are being tackled in a number of ways: Subsidies help smaller farms to continue working, and rural business centers have been created to advise and assist farmers.

▲ This traditional farmhouse near Aurillac in south-central France is surrounded by sunflowers that are grown for their oil.

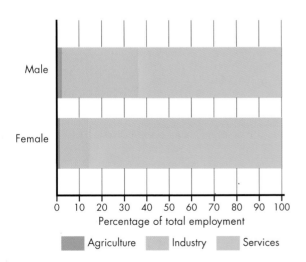

▲ Labor force by sector and gender

Focus on: Women in the Workforce

In France, the number of women who work has increased steadily. The main reason for this is that women are now more likely to continue with employment after they marry and become mothers. Because of improvements in education, by 1998, 44 percent of full-time female workers had academic qualifications at least equal to the *baccalauréat*. In contrast, only 30 percent of male workers in France met this standard. Unemployment, however, is higher among women than men. They are also less likely to be promoted and occupy less than one-third of executive jobs. One reason for this is that women in France are still almost completely responsible for household and family work, so they have less time for paid employment.

CHAPTER 8

Global Connections

Following the end of World War II, France and Germany formed an economic alliance, the European Economic Community, that eventually grew into the European Union. Over the years, France's government has regarded the EU as a way of extending its power, and the country has maintained a strong influence on EU policies. France has resisted moves that might change this, for example, by vetoing Britain's application for EEC membership in the 1960s.

In 2004, the central role of France was challenged by the expansion of EU membership to twenty-five countries. Some people and politicians in France are concerned that elements of France's vision of Europe—for example, the building of a united Europe as a counterbalance to U.S. power—will be lost as a result of EU growth.

THE INVOLVEMENT OF FRANCE IN WORLD AFFAIRS

As one of the top five economically developed countries in the world, France holds a strong position in the global economy. It has trade links with many countries, it influences international politics, and it takes a significant role in world affairs through its membership in a number of international organizations. France is a member of the G8, the group of the eight leading industrialized countries that meets every year to discuss a range of current issues of global significance. Past topics have included the fight against AIDS and the reduction of

▼ The offices of the German company Mercedes-Benz on the Champ Elysees in Paris reflect the close trade links that exist between France and Germany.

debt for many of the world's poorest countries. The G8 was first formed in 1975 by the French president of the time, Valérie Giscard d'Estaing, who invited leaders of the other top five industrial nations—Italy, Britain, the United States, Germany, and Japan—to discuss world affairs in an informal way. Since then, Russia and Canada have joined as permanent members. The president of the European Union also attends G8 meetings, along with guests from other countries who may be invited by any of the member countries.

In 1945, France joined the United Nations. Since then, France has held one of only five permanent seats on the UN Security Council, which is charged with maintaining peace between nations. It was in this forum that, in 2003, France opposed the U.S.-led war on Iraq, arguing that it went against the UN charter.

France wanted to continue using a diplomatic rather than a military approach to disarm Iraq. In other circumstances, France has supported military intervention through the UN. In 2001, for example, France was in favor of sending troops to Afghanistan.

▲ Official visits, such as President Chirac's visit to Tunisia in 1995, help publicize France's global links.

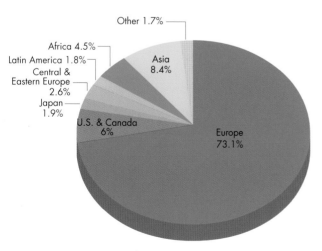

▲ Origin of imports by major trading region

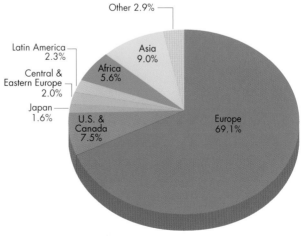

▲ Destination of exports by major trading region

France is also a member of the North Atlantic Treaty Organization. Through this military alliance, French armed forces took part in military intervention in Kosovo in 1999. In 2003, thirty-four thousand troops from France's armed forces were stationed in countries around the world, including former French colonies in Africa, such as the Central African Republic. Most of these troops worked in peacekeeping for the UN.

Alongside the element of international cooperation, France has always maintained an independent foreign policy. This is illustrated by the French approach to the Israeli-Palestinian conflict. France has long insisted that there can be no solution to the conflict without the involvement of the Palestinian leader, including during the period that Yasser Arafat, who died in 2004, held this post.

DEVELOPMENT AID

France is one of the largest donors of development aid in the world. In 2001, France donated 0.37 percent of its gross domestic product to development projects. France gives most of its development aid to its former colonies. In 2002, for example, the top five countries given aid by France were African former colonies, with Côte d'Ivoire receiving the most (13 percent of the total). French companies may also benefit from the money given as aid because

? Did You Know?

France still maintains strong links with countries that used to be French colonies. For many of these countries, France is one of their most important trading partners. For example, Côte d'Ivoire exports coffee and cocoa to France while importing French manufactured goods.

◀ French troops assist an injured comrade in Kosovo in 1999. As a member of NATO, France was part of the military presence in the Balkans during the 1990s conflict.

▲ The world's largest passenger airplane, the Airbus A380—a prototype of which is shown in the background of this picture—has been built in Toulouse, France. The Airbus A380 has two decks and can carry up to 550 passengers.

they are often employed to carry out work on development projects. For example, a French engineering consortium won a contract worth 88 million Euros to electrify train lines in Algeria. France also contributes to UN humanitarian relief operations. In 2004, French military planes were used to transport food supplies to refugees fleeing to Chad from Darfur, Sudan.

Did You Know?

About 165 million people in the world use the French language. French is the official language in more than thirty African countries. Many of these countries, such as Côte d'Ivoire and Senegal, used to be French colonies. Belgium, Switzerland, Luxembourg, and Canada also have French as one of their official languages.

Focus on: France as a Nuclear Power

France has nuclear weapons as part of its national defenses. In 1995, France carried out a series of nuclear tests, setting off underground explosions on Mururoa Atoll in the South Pacific. Mururoa Atoll is part of French Polynesia, a former colonial territory of France that is now politically independent but still economically dependent on France. Numerous local and global protests took place against these tests. The protesters felt that France could be causing considerable damage to the environment. People were also angry that France carried out these potentially damaging tests far away from mainland France. Within French Polynesia, riots and demonstrations took place in Tahiti, and people in Australia, New Zealand, and Japan boycotted French products, such as wine. In 1996, France signed the Comprehensive Test Ban Treaty, which prevents it from conducting more nuclear tests. Since then, French scientists have used computer models to study the effects of nuclear explosions.

CHAPTER 9

Transportation and Communications

▲ Since 1969, most of France's *autoroutes*, or super-highways, have been privately run, and there are now toll booths throughout the network. These roads provide speedy routes for those who pay the tolls.

France has one of the longest road networks in Europe. Of its 555,174 miles (894,000 km) of roads, over 5,592 miles (9,000 km) are super-highway, or autoroute. The majority of France's superhighways are privately-run toll roads. Some of them are given names, such as the Autoroute du Soleil (Highway of the Sun), which links Paris with the warmer Mediterranean regions.

France recognizes the economic importance of good transportation networks and has established excellent road and rail links with other countries. Some of these have demanded considerable feats of engineering. The 32-mile (50-km) long Channel Tunnel runs under the English Channel and links France with Britain. A tunnel cut through the Alpine mountain range of Mont Blanc links France with Italy.

Car ownership is high in France. Over 80 percent of households have one car, and over 30 percent have two or more. Diesel cars account for about one-third of new car sales, a higher

 Did You Know?

Over 76 percent of France's total freight is carried by road. The amount has increased by about 100 percent since the mid-1980s. Over the same period, the amount of freight carried by rail fell by about 25 percent.

proportion than elsewhere in Europe. Diesel vehicles have been popular because they are fuel efficient, but their popularity has declined recently because they produce higher levels of pollutants than nondiesel vehicles. Air pollution is now a major concern in France, particularly in urban areas with high levels of traffic.

RAILROADS

France's rail network extends for 19,993 miles (32,175 km) and includes about 2,796 miles (4,500 km) of specialized track for France's high-speed train service, the Train à Grande Vitesse (TGV). The TGV links France's largest population centers and carries 71 million of the 295 million passengers who travel by rail in France every year. Designed and built by the French, the TGV was the first high-speed train in Europe, and it has significantly cut travel times on major routes. In the 1970s, it used to take six hours to travel between Grenoble and Paris. Today, the same trip takes just three hours.

The TGV has increased average journey speeds from about 74 miles per hour (120 kilometers per hour) to 106 mph (170 kph), with top speeds of over 137 mph (220 kph) on longer journeys. In 1990, the TGV set the world rail speed record for a conventional wheeled train with a speed of 320 mph (515 kph). In spite of these achievements, the TGV has been criticized for being too costly. Environmentalists are concerned that the TGV's specially designed track has had a great impact on the landscape and, in some places, damaged fragile local ecosystems, such as the hills of Provence around Marseille, in southern France.

 Did You Know?
In 1999, the TGV record speed was exceeded by a Japanese experimental magnetic levitation ("maglev") train that reached a speed of 345 mph (581 kph), although the TGV record for conventional wheeled trains still holds.

 Did You Know?
France's wealthiest region, the Île de France, is at the center of the national road and rail networks.

▼ TGV technology has been bought by many countries, including Australia, Taiwan, and Spain.

▲ Charles de Gaulle Airport is one of two international airports that serve Paris. (The other is Orly.) It has three terminal complexes that handle both domestic and international flights.

AIR TRAVEL

Because France is a large country, domestic air travel is important. The country has many small regional airports with domestic flights operating from them, as well as main airports dealing with international flights. Passenger traffic increased by over 250 percent over twenty years. About 4.8 billion tons of freight pass through France's airports each year.

URBAN TRANSIT SYSTEMS

Traffic congestion and air pollution are serious concerns in many of France's cities, particularly in Paris. In Paris, the *métro*, or subway, was first established in 1900 to handle transportation within the city center. Today, the métro carries about nine million passengers daily. Many commuters, however, continue to travel into Paris by car. This is a trend that Régie Autonome des Transports

Parisiens (RATP), the operators of public transportation in Paris, have been trying to reverse for the past thirty years. In 1977, RATP linked the métro with the regional express rail network of trains connecting central Paris with the suburbs. In 1998, a fully automated rail line called the Meteor was added to the métro network. Several cities, including Lille, Lyon, and Marseille, have developed light rail networks to try to reduce traffic congestion in their urban areas.

Did You Know?

The world's highest road bridge—the viaduct de Millau—opened in December 2004. This four-lane bridge crosses 885 feet (270 m) above the Tarn Valley, which lies at the southern edge of the Massif Central, near the town of Millau in the Languedoc region.

FRANCE AND THE INFORMATION SOCIETY

The Internet has been relatively slow to take off in France. The reason for this, in part, is a system called Minitel, established by France Telecom twenty years ago. Minitel gives phone subscribers a terminal to access services through the phone lines, in a way that is similar to the Internet. Many people in France, therefore, saw no need to pay for the personal computers needed for the Internet when they already had free equipment to do many of the same things. Minitel terminals are simpler than a computer, consisting of a small screen and keyboard that is connected to a phone.

In the past ten years, however, a communications revolution has occurred in France, with great growth in the use of the Internet and mobile phones. The number of people in France using

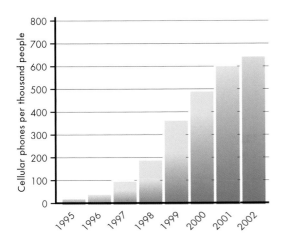

▲ Cellular phone use per 1,000 people, 1995–2002

Transport & Communications Data

- 🗁 Total roads: 555,174 miles/894,000 km
- 🗁 Total paved roads: 555,174 miles/ 894,000 km
- 🗁 Total unpaved roads: 0 miles/0 km
- 🗁 Total railroads: 19,993 miles/32,175 km
- 🗁 Major airports: 477
- 🗁 Cars per 1,000 people: 477
- 🗁 Cellular phones per 1,000 people: 647
- 🗁 Personal computers per 1,000 people: 347
- 🗁 Internet users per 1,000 people: 314

Source: World Bank and CIA World Factbook

the Internet increased from 2.2 million in 1997 to 19 million by 2004, and the number of cellular phone users in the country increased from 0.8 million in 1994 to 39 million in 2004. Networks for both are highly developed in urban areas but less developed in rural areas. The development of information technology is a government priority. In 1997, the Government Action Program for the Information Society was set up. This program has made sure that all secondary schools in France are connected to the Internet.

Focus on: Space Research

France's National Space Center opened in 1961 to provide technical and research expertise to the space industry. It is also a member of the European Space Agency (ESA) and contributes 29 percent of the ESA budget. The space industry accounts for about thirteen thousand jobs on French territory. France also hosts the ESA's launch site at Kouron, in French Guiana. The ESA is not involved with manned spaceflights. It focuses, instead, on launching satellites to advance navigation, communication, the media, and the monitoring of the global environment.

▲ This interactive science park near Toulouse has a life-size model of the European Space Agency's Ariane 5 space rocket.

CHAPTER 10

Education and Health

Education between the ages of six and sixteen has been free and compulsory in France and its territories since 1967. Preschool education for children over three years old had 100 percent attendance in 2000, up from 61 percent in 1970. The value attached to education in French society is reflected by the amount of funding it receives—5.8 percent of the gross domestic product, compared with the EU average of 4.92 percent. About 80 percent of French schools are state-run and secular; most of the remaining 20 percent are private Catholic schools. France has two Muslim schools, one in Lille, in northern France, and the other in Paris.

▼ In France's primary schools, the basic skills of reading, writing, and arithmetic are given high priority.

THE STRUCTURE OF THE EDUCATION SYSTEM

Children in France go to primary school at age six. At the age of eleven, they go to a type of secondary school called a *collège*. A state-run collège takes all children from the local area, regardless of ability or background. At fifteen, students move on to a *lycée*, which may be vocational, technical, or general, depending on

? Did You Know?

Until the 1980s, France's national curriculum required that all children be taught the same subject at the same time regardless of where they lived. The Decentralization Acts in 1982 and 1984 allowed régions, départements, communes, and individual schools a say in the development of their curricula and timetables.

the aptitudes and preferences of the individual students. Those remaining in school until eighteen will have taken the *baccalauréat*, or *le bac*, a program of study first created by Napoleon in 1808. Students choose options within le bac that allow them to specialize in mathematics, science, or philosophy, among other areas, while continuing to study a range of subjects. The number of students completing le bac has risen from 69 percent of those age eighteen in 1970 to over 80 percent in 2001. The baccalauréat qualification is the essential credential for entry into any of France's national universities. The percentage of French students entering higher education has risen sharply, from only 16.8 percent in 1980 to 52.5 percent in 2000.

Instead of going to universities, a few students in France go to *grandes écoles*, which are highly prestigious institutions that require a rigorous entry examination called the *concours*. Students study for the concours at a special lycée. Those who are accepted to the grandes écoles are likely, following graduation, to be recruited for positions in the country's government and top jobs in industry and commerce.

VARIATIONS IN EDUCATIONAL ACHIEVEMENTS

At 99 percent, adult literacy is almost universal in France, but there are some variations that appear to relate to socioeconomic or cultural groups. Immigrant communities, for example, have lower literacy rates, in spite of the fact that education is free to all. France's government has established "priority education areas" to provide extra funds to collèges that serve disadvantaged areas. In 2001, about 18 percent of primary and 21 percent of secondary pupils in France attended collèges in these areas.

▲ In France's collèges, teachers assess the progress of each student at the end of the year and decide whether they move up to the next level.

Education and Health Data

- Life expectancy at birth, male: 75.5
- Life expectancy at birth, female: 83.0
- Infant mortality rate per 1,000: 4
- Under-five mortality rate per 1,000: 6
- Physicians per 1,000 people: 3.3
- Health expenditure as % of GDP: 9.6%
- Education expenditure as % of GDP: 5.8%
- Primary school net enrollment: 100%
- Student-teacher ratio, primary school: 18.7
- Adult literacy % age 15+: 99

Source: United Nations Agencies and World Bank

HEALTH

In 2000, the World Health Organization said that France had the best health-care system in the world. The level of satisfaction is high, with 66 percent of French people reporting they are happy with the care they received (compared with 40 percent in Britain). The country has 3 doctors for every 1,000 people (compared with 3 for every 1,800 people in Britain and 3 for every 2,700 people in the United States). Their success in treating cancer and heart disease is impressive, with survival rates higher than in other European countries. Because of this top-class health-care system, life expectancy at birth for French women was 83 years in 2004 (second to Japan); for French men, it was 75.5 years.

Until 2004, French citizens could choose to see specialists without first seeing a primary doctor, and there were no waiting lists for treatment in hospitals. Medical costs were covered by a combination of the state's social security system and *mutuelles,* or cooperative insurance bodies.

Although France spends over 9 percent of its GDP on health care, the country has a health-care budget deficit of over ten billion Euros a year that is predicted to increase. As the aging population puts more pressure on the system, the projected deficit for 2010 is twenty-nine billion Euros. In spite of public opposition to changes in the health-care system, reforms were enacted in 2004 with the hope of reducing the deficit by 2007. Patients now have to pay for some medical tests, prescriptions, and visits to a specialist.

▼ France has some excellent medical research facilities, such as this gene-research center at Evry, which is located near Paris.

LIFESTYLE CHOICES

Some of France's most serious health problems are linked to some of its people's lifestyle choices, such as drinking alcohol and smoking. French men have the highest level of cancer-related deaths in western Europe, and deaths caused by cancer increased from 20 percent of all deaths in 1970 to nearly 28 percent by 1999. The death rate from heart disease decreased slightly over the same period, but it is still considered to be too high. The government has increased taxes on cigarettes and launched campaigns to discourage people from smoking and drinking. Another health problem that has increased in France is obesity, which is associated with poor diets that involve more fast food and less fresh produce.

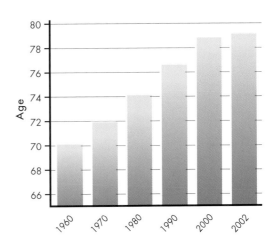

▲ Life expectancy at birth, 1960–2002

▶ The small markets that are held weekly in many towns and villages in France are good places to buy fresh fruit and vegetables. They are now challenged, however, by the increased availability of packaged foods.

Focus on: The Pasteur Institute, Paris

The Pasteur Institute is one of the world's leading medical research centers, employing over one thousand scientists. Louis Pasteur, who is famous for discovering the sterilization process and the vaccine for rabies, first established the institute as a nonprofit research organization in 1887. Since then, eight of the institute's scientists have been awarded the Nobel Prize for Medicine. The institute has been responsible for the discovery of several vaccines, including those for diphtheria, tetanus, and tuberculosis. In 1983, scientists from the Pasteur Institute were the first to isolate the AIDS virus. The institute's research into HIV/AIDS continues today, benefiting not only the 0.3 percent of adults between ages fifteen and forty-nine in France who are affected by the virus but also the millions of people in developing countries who are affected by it.

CHAPTER 11

Culture and Religion

▲ Traditional French cuisine uses fresh ingredients that are produced locally. In coastal areas, shellfish are used in regional speciality dishes.

French cuisine has a worldwide reputation for high quality and for delicacies such as cheeses, baguettes, crêpes, and patés. The word "gourmet" means a person who enjoys good food and drink. The word originates from France, and most French people are indeed true gourmets. The French love of food can be seen in their use of good quality, fresh ingredients and in their shopping for food in local markets. Until recently, sitting down to a four-course meal each day was normal. A 2004 government survey shows that this habit is changing, with 55 percent of those interviewed eating a smaller evening meal in front of the TV. The French habit of drinking *vin de table*, or table wine, with every meal is also changing: in 1980, 454 million quarts (430 million liters) of wine were consumed, a figure that had declined to about 360 million quarts (340 million liters) by 2003.

THE VISUAL ARTS

France has played an important role in the history of Western art. In the fourteenth century, during the Renaissance, French kings invited the finest European artists to decorate their palaces. Paris became the center of important artistic developments, although the artists themselves working there were not necessarily French. In the nineteenth century, a distinctly French art movement called Impressionism had a far-reaching influence. Impressionist artists, including Edouard Manet

(1832–1883) and Claude Monet (1840–1926), tried to escape the unmoving look of the art of the time by creating the appearance of reflected light in their paintings. Other famous French artists included the post-Impressionist Henri Toulouse-Lautrec (1864–1901), who painted scenes from Parisian cafés, and the Cubist painter Georges Braques (1882–1963). Today France has some of the world's best art museums. The Louvre museum in Paris was visited by 6.6 million people in 2004.

Going to the movies is more popular in France than anywhere else in Europe. The popularity of movies in France dates back to 1895, when the world's first public movie theater opened in Paris. Today, the French film industry is thriving, largely because it receives public subsidies of more than 245 million Euros a year. Many French directors, actors, and actresses—for example, Audrey Tautou, Gerard Depardieu, and Isabel Huppert—are world famous. One of the most famous international film festivals is held every year in Cannes, which is located in southeastern France.

France has also contributed to the development of photography. In 1826, Joseph Nicéphore Niépce was the first person to produce a photographic image on paper. The image took eight hours to develop. In 1839, Jacque Daguerre reduced the development time for photographs to half an hour.

? Did You Know?

The value that is attached to movies in French culture is reflected in the development of Futuroscope, a unique theme park about movies, video, and visual technology, that was opened near Poitiers in 1987. Futuroscope now attracts about two million visitors a year.

▼ The striking glass pyramid that covers the main entrance of the Louvre museum in Paris was designed by the Chinese-born architect Leoh Ming Pei.

ARCHITECTURE

France has a fascinating variety of architecture. There are wonderful examples of Gothic cathedrals, which are characterized by pointed arches, flying buttresses, and stained-glass windows, that were built between the twelfth and fifteenth centuries. Notre Dame Cathedral in Paris, completed in about 1345, has spectacular rose windows and ornate flying buttresses. The chateaus of the Loire Valley are examples of lavishly decorated royal country retreats from the fifteenth and sixteenth centuries. Modern architects have also made their mark, particularly in Paris, with structures such as the Pompidou Centre, built in the 1970s.

FRENCH WRITERS

There is a long tradition in France of writers tackling philosophical questions and ideas. The work of René Descartes (1596–1660) marks the beginning of modern philosophy and has influenced philosophers around the world. Other philosophers who have had a worldwide influence include Jean-Paul Sartre (1905–1980), Simone de Beauvoir (1908–1986), and Jacques Derrida (1930–2004). French writers have also produced famous novels, many of which are today considered classics. Examples of these works include *Les Miserables,* by Victor Hugo (1802–1885), and *L'Estranger,* by Albert Camus (1913–1960).

▶The Pompidou Center in Paris is designed to have its pipes and ducts on the outside, giving it an unusual and controversial appearance.

RELIGION IN A SECULAR STATE

In France, the separation of religion and state—called the secular principle—was established in 1905 and further developed in 1946, when it first appeared in the country's constitution. Religion is considered to be a matter of personal choice, and people in France are allowed to practice whatever religion they believe, but the country itself is to have no official religion. In recent years, tensions between ethnic groups with different religious beliefs have put the secular principle under pressure. France has

churches in every city, town, and village, reflecting the historical importance of religion, particularly Catholicism, in the country. About 65.5 percent of the population is Catholic, although fewer than one out of ten go to Mass regularly. Immigrants from North Africa, a region that is mainly Islamic, brought their faith with them when they settled in France. Muslims are now France's second-largest religious group, making up approximately 7.1 percent of the country's population. Protestants make up about 1.2 percent. Jews make up about 1 percent—a higher proportion than in any other western European country.

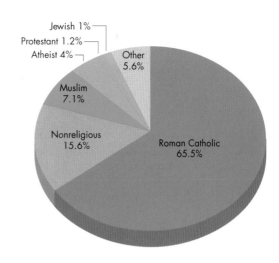

▲ France's major religions

Focus on: Defense of the Secular Principle or Racism?

In September 2004, a new law was passed in France banning school students and those who work in the government's public services from wearing obvious religious symbols, including large crucifixes, turbans, and headscarves. Supporters of the law say it ensures that schools and state institutions, such as the courts, remain secular places, unaffected by religious and cultural beliefs. Opponents, however, see it as a racist law that targets Muslim girls, whose headscarves are a particularly obvious religious symbol that cannot easily be substituted with something smaller and less obtrusive. They point to the fact that Catholic students are still able to wear small crucifixes. Many Muslims feel they are being forced to choose whether they are Muslim or French. They believe the ban will encourage discrimination against Muslims.

? Did You Know?

In France's secular school system, students study philosophy instead of studying religion.

► France has about sixteen hundred mosques and Muslim prayer halls. Most of them, however, are small, makeshift facilities, not large buildings like this one in Paris.

CHAPTER 12

Leisure and Tourism

The thirty-five-hour working week introduced in 1997 led to a considerable increase in leisure time for many French employees. Leisure interests account for about 10 percent of household spending in France today. The French enjoy a wide variety of leisure activities, including reading, watching TV, and, increasingly, using personal computers (PCs). In 2003, about 50 percent of French homes had a PC, compared with 80 percent in Sweden and 66 percent in Britain. Increasing numbers of PCs are being sold in France, and French companies are now creating and marketing PC games.

▼ *Pétanque,* or *boules,* is the fourth most popular sport in France. Many local variations of this traditional game are played around the country.

Traditionally, the family has been a focus of leisure time in France, with friends and family frequently gathering to cook and enjoy meals. Although gatherings for Sunday lunches and special occasions are still popular, there has been a decline in the number of people spending time in this way during the week. French families also enjoy eating out. In the past, the country had many small family-run restaurants that welcomed families and offered delicious food. These are now under threat from the spread of fast-food chains, and many small restaurants in France have closed.

Outside the home, many French people take part in sports. A survey in 2002 revealed that 66 percent of men and 50 percent of women

▲ The wide beaches along the coast near Le Havre, in northern France, are used for sand-yacht racing.

participate in a sporting activity. Popular sports include soccer, tennis, basketball, and judo. The traditional game of *pétanque* (or *boules,* as it is known in some regions of France) is still popular, particularly among the older generation, and most towns and villages have open-air public areas for the playing of this game. A number of internationally famous sporting events take place in France every year. These include the French Open Tennis Championship and the twenty-four-hour motor racing event at Le Mans (*24 heures du Mans*), which was first run in the 1920s. France also hosts the most famous bicycle race in the world, the Tour de France, which attracts more than two hundred entrants. This race first started in 1903, and it takes place over a three-week period in July. Each year its route changes, visiting different regions of France and sometimes a neighboring country for a day or two. It always finishes, however, along the Champs Elysee in Paris. The Tour de France is extremely grueling because it covers a distance of over 2,000 miles (3,200 km) and includes steep climbs and descents in mountainous areas such as the Alps and the Massif Central.

 Did You Know?

The Paris-Dakar Rally is a long-distance race of over 6,214 miles (10,000 km) for motorcycles, cars, and trucks. It has been run every year since 1978. Although referred to as the Paris-Dakar Rally, the route occasionally varies, with other European towns hosting the start. Dakar, the ending point, is in Senegal. First created by a Frenchman, Thierry Sabine, the rally now has people from over forty nations taking part, although the majority who enter are French.

▲ French beaches get very crowded, particularly during the month of August, when the country's schools have their long summer break.

THE FRENCH ON VACATION

Taking a long summer break in August while the schools are closed is a French tradition. Most French people stay in France for their vacations; only 10 percent go abroad. This percentage is low compared to the Germans and British, of whom 50 and 33 percent respectively vacation abroad, but it is higher than that of Americans, of whom only 4 percent vacation outside the United States. France offers many natural, historical, and cultural attractions to tourists. Seaside vacations are particularly popular during the warm summers and have been popular since the eighteenth century, when they were taken to recover from illness. Key resorts in France include Biarritz, on the southern Atlantic coast, and Nice, on the Mediterranean coast. Winter resorts popular for skiing and snowboarding include Méribel, in the French Alps, and Les Monts Dore, in the Massif Central. Few French people take package holidays, preferring instead to stay with friends or family. Camping also is popular in France, especially during the long summer vacations, because it is a cheap and convenient vacation for families. Many towns and villages in France have a municipal campsite, and there are hundreds of sites in popular holiday areas such as the Mediterranean coast. In addition, France has the highest rate of second home ownership in Europe.

FOREIGN TOURISTS IN FRANCE

With more than 77 million foreign tourists traveling to France each year, tourism is important for the country's economy and is the main source of income in some rural areas, such as the Massif Central. France offers tourists an enormous range of attractions, including historical sites such as the Eiffel Tower, which attracts more than six million visitors a year; theme parks such as Disneyland Paris, which has about twelve million visitors a year; and areas of great natural and scenic beauty, such as the Gorge du Tarn. Mont-Saint-Michel combines historic and natural appeal, and it is one of the most visited sights outside Paris, receiving up to 3.5 million visitors each year.

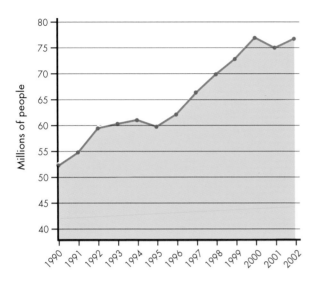

▲ Changes in international tourism, 1990–2002

Tourism in France

📂 Tourist arrivals, millions: 77
📂 Earnings from tourism in U.S.$:
   32,329,000,000
📂 Tourism as % foreign earnings: 5
📂 Tourist departures, millions: 17.4
📂 Expenditure on tourism in U.S.$:
   19,460,000,000

Source: World Bank

Focus on: The Alps

Tourism in the Alps is a multibillion dollar industry. During winter, people come to the Alps to ski, often staying in specially-built resorts such as the Alps d'Huez, in the Parc National des Écrins, a national park. In the summer, many come to hike and climb. There may be up to three hundred people climbing Mont Blanc on a single day. Since the late 1980s, there have been concerns that this industry is threatened by global warming. Less snow has fallen, particularly on the slopes below 6,562 feet (2,000 m), and snowfalls have been occurring in February rather than in December. Higher temperatures in the summer months have melted ice high in the peaks, leading to increased risk of rock falls that are dangerous to hikers. Some scientists believe that these recent changes are the result of natural variations in the world's climate rather than global warming.

▼ Tourists enjoy a barge vacation on the Canal du Midi at Olonzac, near Béziers.

CHAPTER 13

Environment and Conservation

France's natural landscape supports a variety of habitats and an impressive range of plant and animal species. The country has more than 4,600 species of flowering plants, 283 types of birds, and 93 species of mammals—more than in any other European country. Many of the habitats that support these species, however, have been damaged or destroyed by human activities such as the development of new transportation links and the expansion of farmland. Several species, including wolves and brown bears, are currently endangered in France. The Pyrenees ibex and the Corsican deer are already extinct. France has undertaken and continues to develop a variety of measures to protect its environment.

PARKS AND NATURE RESERVES

France has four types of protected areas that make up 11.3 percent of its land. *Parcs nationaux* (national parks), of which there were seven in 2003, and *parcs naturels regionaux* (regional natural parks) have been created in areas of natural beauty that are sparsely populated. One example is the Parc Naturel des Cévennes, which covers 352 sq miles (912 sq km) in the Languedoc-Roussillon region. These parks aim to balance conservation with the needs of the people who live in them. *Reserves naturelles* (nature reserves), of which there were 144 in 2001, and *reserves biologiques* (biological reserves) are smaller in area and focus on preserving specific ecosystems. They are often located within larger protected areas. For example, the Scandola nature reserve covers just over 7 sq miles (18 sq km) within the Parc Naturel Regional de la Corse in Corsica.

WETLANDS

In addition to administering France's official protected areas, the country's Ministry of the Environment has special powers to enforce the protection of especially threatened habitats. For example, between 1960 and 1995 over half of France's wetlands had disappeared, so the ministry set up the national Action Plan for Wetlands in 1995. Wetlands cover 7,722 sq miles (20,000 sq km) of France, and the plan provides national guidelines on how they can be better managed and conserved. The

◀ The beautiful limestone scenery of the Gorge du Tarn is one of the natural features that is protected in the Parc Natural des Cévennes.

Camargue, a fine example of wetland in southern France, is at risk from agricultural pesticides, water-borne industrial pollution, and pressure from more than one million tourists who visit the area each year. The Camargue is also a *parc naturel regionaux* that is home to more than 1,000 species of flowering plants, 50 species of fish, 15 types of reptile, and many species of birds, including flamingos.

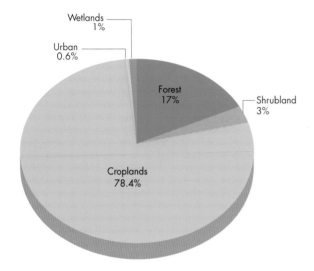

▲ Habitat type as percentage of total area

▲ A grassland fire is doused with water. Grassland and forest fires have become more frequent in some rural areas of France, such as this part of Provence.

Environmental and Conservation Data

🗁 Forested area as % of total land area: 17
🗁 Protected area as % of total land area: 11.3
🗁 Number of protected areas: 1,153

SPECIES DIVERSITY

Category	Known species	Threatened species
Mammals	93	18
Breeding birds	283	5
Reptiles	46	3
Amphibians	39	2
Fish	169	5
Plants	4,630	2

Source: World Resources Institute

▲ Trees have been cleared from this slope to make way for a ski slope. In the summer, the bare slope is prone to erosion because it does not have the protection of its natural vegetation.

FORESTS

Forests and woodlands cover approximately 22.9 million acres (9.3 million ha) of France. They are threatened by a range of activities and problems, including commercial logging and damage from acid rain. Acid rain, in particular, is a problem in the north, where there is a higher concentration of industries. Since the 1980s, the government of France has passed legislation to ensure that industries pay to clean up the pollution they cause. This policy is known as the "polluter pays" principle, and it has been successful in helping to reduce and control industrial air and water pollution.

MOUNTAIN REGIONS

Mountainous and alpine environments are fragile, with thin soils and steep slopes that are prone to erosion. They are easily damaged by the development of skiing facilities, such as ski lifts, special ski runs, and hotels, all of which involve cutting down many trees. Developments such as these not only cause direct destruction of wildlife habitats and plants—some of which are only found in a very few areas—but they can also lead to increased risk of landslides, avalanches, and floods. In 1991, France joined with five other Alpine countries to draw up the Convention for the Protection of the Alps to try to limit the damage. In 1997, it was agreed that, under this convention, no new ski resorts would be built in the Alps, although there were no restrictions imposed on the expansion of existing ski resorts.

ENVIRONMENTAL DILEMMAS

Poor air quality in urban areas is a growing problem in France. Emissions from vehicles are the major source of air pollution in France. In Paris, about three million cars enter the capital daily, many of which have diesel engines that emit high levels of pollutants. On some days, a photochemical smog is produced when exhaust emissions react with sunlight. This smog causes a rise in health problems, such as asthma and bronchial infections. In an attempt to tackle this problem, France's government promotes the annual European Car-Free Day and the introduction of low-sulphur diesel fuel that reduces sulphur dioxide emissions by 90 percent.

Emissions of greenhouse gases, such as carbon dioxide (CO_2), have been significantly reduced in France largely because nuclear energy has been used to generate 81 percent of the country's electricity. Some environmentalists, however, are concerned about the long-term effects of using nuclear energy. Nuclear waste products, although extremely small in quantity, remain hazardous for many years and have to be disposed of very carefully.

▲ The spraying of pesticides and herbicides on agricultural land leads to many environmental problems, including the pollution of rivers with chemicals that are washed into them by rain.

Did You Know?

In France, sulphur dioxide (SO_2) emissions fell by 72 percent between 1980 and 2000. Carbon dioxide (CO_2) emissions fell by 20 percent in the same period.

Focus on: The Return of Wolves to the French Alps

European wolves were once extinct in France but can now be found in the country again, roaming areas of the Alps. In the early 1990s, a wolf pack wandered from Italy into the French Alps. By 2004, there were about fifty-five wolves in ten packs living in the area between the Italian border and the Rhône Valley. The wolves are a protected species, but their return has not been welcomed by all. Wolves have attacked and killed increasing numbers of sheep—192 killed in 1994, rising to more than two thousand in 2002. France's government has subsidized the employment of more shepherds and the use of more guard dogs. These measures have reduced the killings since 2002. Farmers, however, say the cost of protecting their livestock from the wolves is too high, even with government help. They are demanding the right to shoot wolves on sight.

CHAPTER 14

Future Challenges

Increasing social tensions and religious differences are seen by some as the most pressing problem that France faces. Young people of the urban "sink estates," where many with immigrant backgrounds live, are increasingly angry about their poor quality of life, which they believe is a result of racial discrimination. Other members of French society fear that this anger is directed against the republican values of French society. Among some of these people, there has been a rise in the popularity of extreme right-wing parties with racist policies. The considerable support that the Front National received in the presidential elections of 2002 shocked many French people.

▼ Many of France's high-rise urban developments, such as this one in Paris, have become very run down since they were built in the 1950s.

Support for this group, however, is likely to increase if issues of inequality between different ethnic communities in France and the anger that they generate are not tackled.

Like some other economically developed countries, France faces the challenge of an aging population. With a low birth rate and a high life expectancy, the proportion of the French population over the age of sixty-five is increasing. Within the next fifteen years, this may cause pension problems and increase the tax burden on the economically active younger members of French society. French productivity, however, is high and, if it continues to rise, these problems may be avoided. The aging population, however, will increase the burden on France's health-care system, which some leaders already think is costing the country too much.

▲ Members of Greenpeace stage an antinuclear protest during a conference on climate change in Lyon. Their banner says, "Nuclear energy is not the answer to the greenhouse effect."

HEALTH PROBLEMS

The French government has launched campaigns aimed at the prevention of health problems related to the country's current high consumption of tobacco and alcohol. The policies already in place to discourage smoking include larger health warnings on cigarette packs and tax increases to push up the price of cigarettes.

As one of the leading industrial nations in the world, France needs to carefully consider the environmental impact of its economic activities and its high level of energy consumption. Although France's greenhouse gas emissions are considerably lower than most other economically developed nations, France achieves this through heavy dependency on nuclear energy. Fears about the safety of using nuclear energy are increasing among the French public. These fears are causing the government to reconsider the role of nuclear power as a major energy source.

THE FUTURE OF EUROPE

As one of the founding members of the EU, France has had considerable influence on its nature and direction. With the EU's continuing expansion, there are fears that new member countries may only be interested in the economic benefits of the EU free-trade area and will challenge the French vision of a politically integrated Europe. Even the use of French as the EU's main language is threatened, because about 70 percent of the EU new members have English as their second language. It seems that concern about the future direction of the EU has reduced France's support for it. France's rejection of the new EU constitution in May 2005 caused great debate in all EU countries about what EU membership should mean. It will be interesting to see how France—a country that, historically, has had strong political and cultural influences on the world—deals with these issues.

Time Line

15,000 B.C. Cave paintings found in southwestern France provide evidence of early human settlers.

1500 B.C. The Gauls, Celtic people from central Europe, invade France.

52 B.C. The Romans defeat the Gauls.

A.D. 400–500 The Romans are defeated by the Franks.

A.D. 771–814 The rule of Charlemagne, during which the French Empire expands into parts of Spain, Italy, and Germany.

1066 William of Normandy invades England and takes control of areas of France under English rule.

1337–1453 The Hundred Years' War between France and England.

1789 The French Revolution begins with the storming of the Bastille in Paris.

1799 Napoléon Bonaparte comes to power.

1914–1918 During World War I, France is invaded by German troops; much of the fighting takes place on French territory.

1940 During the World War II, France is occupied by Germany until liberated by Allied forces in 1944.

1951 France and Germany form the European Coal and Steel Community, which later becomes the European Economic Community.

1975 French president Valérie Giscard d'Estaing forms a group of the six leading industrial nations called the G6 (now the G8) to discuss world issues.

1990 The French high-speed train sets the world speed record for conventional wheeled trains.

1993 The European Economic Community becomes the European Union.

1995 The French government carries out nuclear testing in the Pacific. Demonstrations take place in many countries against this action.

1996 France signs the Comprehensive Test Ban Treaty and replaces nuclear testing in the Pacific with computer simulations.

1998 France wins the World Cup.

2002 France drops its currency—the franc—in favor of the euro, the common currency of the European Union.

2003 France opposes the invasion of Iraq, arguing for diplomatic rather than military means to deal with the situation.

2004 The highest bridge in the world is constructed in southern France.

2005 In a national referendum, French voters reject the proposed European Union constitution.

Airbus, the European aerospace industry, which is based in France, launches the A380, the world's largest passenger jet.

Glossary

absolute rule a form of government in which the ruler has complete power

Allies the countries, including France, Britain, Canada, and the United States, that fought against Germany, Italy, and Japan in World War II

arrondisement in France's local government, a subdivision of a département

assimilation the taking on by immigrant of the cultural beliefs and practices of his or her new country

baccalauréat an exam taken by French high school students when they are eighteen that is required for entry to a university; also called *le bac*

biomass an energy source derived from organic matter, such as wood or sewage, that can be burned to produce heat

BTU British Thermal Unit, a standard unit of energy

canton in France's local government, a grouping of communes within an arrondisement

climatologist a scientist who specializes in the study of the climate

colonist a person living in a country controlled by another more powerful country and who originally came from that more powerful country

commune the lowest tier of France's local government

consortium an organization of businesses joining together for a shared purpose

constitution the basic political principles by which a state is governed

coup a sudden seizing of political power by a group of people, often led by the military

crêpes pancakes made from eggs and flour, served with either savory or sweet fillings

delta a natural geographic feature that occurs where a river deposits its load of sediment at its mouth

democracy a system of government under which citizens are able to vote for representatives in the government

département the second level of France's local government after the régions

dynasty a series of rulers from the same family

ecosystem all the living things in an area and the physical environment in which they exist

elite the most powerful group in a society

flying buttress the part of the external structure of Gothic cathedrals designed to support the weight of the walls and ceiling and allow the interior to be free of pillars

Free French French people who fought against German rule during the occupation of France during World War II

global warming a gradual increase in world temperatures caused by greenhouse gases

gross domestic income (GDI) total income earned from industries in a country and exports produced there

gross domestic product (GDP) the total value of the goods and services produced in a country in a given year

gross national income (GNI) a country's gross domestic product plus the net income it earns from investments in other countries in a given year; also called gross national product (GNP)

left-wing having to do with the set of political beliefs that usually favors government reform and the use of government power to control the distribution of wealth

National Assembly the lower house of the French parliament (the upper house is the Senate) consisting of 577 elected members, called deputies, each of whom represents an area of France

racist having to do with the idea that other races are not as good as one's own; also, a person who holds such beliefs

republic a country governed by elected representatives of the people and headed by a president

right-wing having to do with the set of political beliefs that usually favors traditional government policies and resistance to government reform or change

secular nonreligious

service industries industries or businesses, such as shops, insurance companies, transportation companies, and tourist attractions, that provide services or sell goods to people or other industries.

subsidies money given by a government to support an industry when it has difficulty in making enough through its own efforts

United Nations (UN) an international organization established after World War II in 1945 to work toward the maintaining of international peace and security and international economic and social cooperation

vetoing blocking or overturning a vote in a meeting

Further Information

BOOKS TO READ

The Cooking of France *(Superchef* series)
Matthew Locricchio
(Benchmark Books)

D-Day *(Days That Changed the World* series)
Colin Hynson
(World Almanac Library)

Eiffel Tower *(Building World Landmarks* series)
Meg Greene
(Blackbirch Press)

European Union *(International Organizations* series)
Petra Press
(World Almanac Library)

France *(Enchantment of the World* series)
Don Nardo
(Scholastic Library Publishing)

The French Revolution
Adrian Gilbert
(Sea to Sea Publications)

The Napoleonic Wars: Defeat of the Grand Army
(History's Great Defeats series)
Thomas Streissguth
(Lucent Books)

Paris *(Great Cities of the World* series)
Gill Stacey
(World Almanac Library)

Versailles *(Places in History* series)
Anthony Mason
(World Almanac Library)

USEFUL WEB SITE

Earth Trends
www.earthtrends.org/

The Economist
www.economist.com/countries/France/

Embassy of France in the United States
www.info-france-usa.org/

The French Revolution
campus.northpark.edu/history/WebChron/
WestEurope/FrenchRev.html

On the Line: Virtual Journey of France
www.oxfam.org.uk/coolplanet/ontheline/explore/
journey/france/frindex.htm

Paris Pages: Culture
www.paris.org/culture.html

Tour de France in 80 Stages
www.diplomatie.gouv.fr/index.gb.html

Underwater Archaeology
www.culture.gouv.fr/culture/archeosm/en/

The World Factbook
www.odci.gov/cia/publications/factbook/geos/
fr.html

The Eiffel Tower
www.tour-eiffel.fr/teiffel/uk/

Index

Page numbers in **bold** indicate pictures.